MIND YOUR
INHERITANCE

VICTOR E. K. MURIITHI

LWAM Resources
info@lwam.org; www.lwam.org
info@vekmuriithi.com; www.vekmuriithi.com

First Published in Great Britain in April 2018

ISBN-13: 978-1986768733
ISBN-10: 1986768732

Table of Contents

Dedication

I dedicate this book to every child of God, i.e. heirs of God and co-heirs with Christ.

Acknowledgements

First and foremost I would like to give thanks to the almighty God for his call upon my life, divine revelation, inspiration and the ability to coherently put together this book.

Most of my research, reading and writing work occurrs on weekends, nights, while on vacation, and other times inconvenient to my family. I want to thank my wife, Emma, for all of the support she has given me. She has been my inspiration and motivation for continuing to improve my knowledge and move my authorship forward. My son, Kirk-Karsten, who is four at the time of writing, has also needed to show patience when his dad was working on this book. I thank God for him and I hope that one day he will read this book and understand why I spent so much time in front of my computer.

I wish to thank my parents, Rev James & Mrs Ruth Muriithi my brothers Daniel & John, my sister Faith and my in-laws for their constant support. Thank you for encouraging me and for praying for me ceaselessly.

I am indebted to Pastor Dishon and entire Mitcham Kingdom Love Church family for recognising and allowing me to exercise my gift and calling. I am grateful for the opportunity to serve in the pastoral team and I hope that the entire family will find this book useful.

Thanks to my editor, Maureen, for editing and proofreading the manuscript and for putting up with my poor punctuation and grammar.

I also wish to thank my 'partners in crime' – fellow ministers of the Gospel, my yokefellows and co-labourers in our Lord's vineyard as well as my bigger family in Sussex (Betty, Alex, Yeunnah and Gadiel) who in one way or another contributed to the completion of this book.May the almighty God richly bless you.

MIND YOUR INHERITANCE

"We have obtained an inheritance, having been predestined according to His purpose who works all things after the counsel of His will, to the end that we who were the first to hope in Christ would be to the praise of His glory. In Him, you also, after listening to the message of truth, the gospel of your salvation—having also believed, you were sealed in Him with the Holy Spirit of promise, who is given as a pledge of our inheritance, with a view to the redemption of God's own possession, to the praise of His glory."

Ephesians 1:11 – 14

The Bible describes our relationship with God as that of a father and his children. As many as receive Christ, to them God gives the right to become his children, even to those who believe in his name. They become born again, not of blood nor of the will of the flesh nor of the will of man, but of God (John 1:12-13).

As God's children, we then have the right to inherit from our Father. Since we know that Jesus died for us, the Bible assures us that we will inherit the same eternal Kingdom that Christ inherited. The Spirit himself testifies with our spirit that we are God's children. If we are children, then we are heirs of God and co-heirs with Christ, if indeed we share in his sufferings in order that we may also share in his glory (Romans 6:16-17).

The Bible says that because we are God's children, he has sent the Spirit of his Son into our hearts, prompting us to call out, 'Abba, Father.' We are God's own children and he has made us his heirs (Galatians 4:6-7).

The Bible is full of references to the inheritance believers have in Christ. Because we are united with Christ, we have received an inheritance from God, for he chose us in advance, and he makes everything work out according to his plan (Ephesians 1:11). Our inheritance is eternal and can never perish, spoil or fade. Our inheritance is stored in heaven for us (Hebrews 9:15; 1 Peter 1:4).

In one of his psalms, David helps us understand that our inheritance is wonderful and delightful. He says in Psalms 16:6, "LORD, you alone are my inheritance, my cup of blessing. You guard all that is mine. The boundary lines have fallen for me in pleasant places; surely I have a delightful inheritance."

Our inheritance is the sum total of all God has promised us in salvation. We are partakers of His riches, His grace, His kindness, His patience, His glory His wisdom, His power and His mercy" (Ephesians 1:7; Romans 2:4; 9:23; 11:33; Ephesians 3:16; 2:4). Although we enjoy many blessings as children of God here on earth, we also have an eternal inheritance reserved for us in heaven.

The Holy Spirit guarantees that we will receive our inheritance. He is God's guarantee that God will give us the inheritance he promised and that he has purchased us to be his own people. God did this so we would praise and glorify him (Ephesians 1:14).

In the New Testament, we see in the gospels as well as in the epistles a few of Jewish inheritance practices being used analogically as a metaphor or as a direct illustration of our spiritual inheritance in Christ. In Galatians 3:15 the Bible says that once a man's will has been ratified, no one can annul it or add to it. And in Galatians 4:1-2 we see that the estate of a child who is a minor is under guardians and trustees until the date set by the father.

In this book, I wish to give you few keys to help you not miss out on your inheritance. Be blessed as you read.

HONOUR YOUR FATHER

> *"I will honour those who honour Me, but those who despise Me will be disgraced."*
>
> *1 Samuel 2:30*

The Bible records two stories where two sons dishonoured their respective fathers in odious terms. Reuben, the eldest son of Jacob, and Absalom, the eldest of David's living children, and next in line in succession to the throne. These two stories carry with them vital teachings on how to lose [not] our inheritance. Reuben lost his inheritance because he dishonoured his father Jacob who was the source of his inheritance. Likewise, Absalom dishonoured his father, disregarded God, and as a result went to the grave in shame.

Before we catechise these stories, it is important to understand the meaning of the word "father". According to Easton's Bible Dictionary, the word "father" means the author or beginner of anything. According to Strong's Concordance, the Greek word used in the New Testament is *"patér"*. This refers to a begetter, originator or a progenitor. Therefore, wherever the scriptures speak of a father, they allude to the source, the originator or transmitter of the thing in question.

Reuben

Back to Reuben and Jacob, the narrative has it that a strange spirit came upon Reuben, and he went had sexual activity with Bilhah, his step-mother's maid and father's concubine. Jacob heard about it and said nothing. (Genesis 35:22). Nothing was heard about it again for many years, and we never heard that Reuben asked for forgiveness or repented or became sober about it. And the matter presumably died just like that. So many events came after it, and nobody mentioned it again. Reuben went with the rest of Jacob's children to Egypt; he saw the glories of Egypt. He was welcomed into the palace of Joseph and ate with him in the royal palace. He grew and had many children and everything was going fine for him. Until the day their father would say the last prayers for them and give them his final decree. Reuben's act with Bilhah was never a secret, but some forty years would pass before Jacob mentioned anything about it.

On his deathbed, Jacob gathered his family together for the final blessing and began to bless them all. But he began with Reuben, the first son, who was to be the heir who should carry the highest blessings among the children. He declared that "Reuben, you are my firstborn; my might and the beginning of my strength, Preeminent in dignity and preeminent in power. Uncontrolled as water, you shall not have pre-eminence, because you went up to your father's bed; Then you defiled it-- he went up to my couch." (Genesis 49:4-5)

The record was opened to his long forgotten atrocity. He thought it had been swept under the carpet. He thought he was smart and had had his fun. Reuben's behaviour angered Jacob to the extent that he gave Reuben's birthright (as firstborn) to Joseph. (1 Chronicles 5:1). The birthright included the right of his descendants (the tribe of Reuben) to become ruler over the tribes (transferred to Judah) and priests (transferred to Levi). Thus, Reuben lost inheritance, priesthood and leadership.

As the eldest son, Reuben was already entitled to half his father's inheritance, and his remaining brothers would share the other half. The firstborn is often called the first sign of his father's strength in the Scriptures. (Deuteronomy 21:7; Psalm 78:51). As the first born, the beginning of Jacob's strength, Reuben was supposed to be an epitome of excellence, dignity and power. He was to be naturally blessed and was born to be a man of natural dignity and power, but his inheritance and his destiny was aborted the day he dishonoured his father.

We see something of the future of the Reubenites in the book of Numbers being small and non-influential. Jacob's sad prophecy for Reuben certainly came true. No judge, prophet, ruler, or prince came from that tribe or any person of prominence except Dathan and Abiram, who were noted for their rebellion against Moses. In the first census, the tribe of Reuben was numbered at 46,500. But in the second census, the tribe had decreased to 43,730. The prayer of Moses in Deuteronomy 33:6 said: "Let Reuben live and not die, nor his men be few." Moses had to intercede on behalf of the tribe of Reuben, so that they would not disappear.

God is deserving of the highest honour because of both who He is and what He has done. It is in Him that we live and move and have our being (Acts 17:28). All that we have, we have received from Him. All things have been made by Him and for Him. We can only honour God if we live, not for our own glory, but for His glory. He is worthy of all honour.

Many people dishonour God and continue living as normal, but the truth is: long after a very hot pressing iron had been disconnected from the power source; it would still be hot for a while, until it begins to grow cold. When we dishonour our heavenly father by sabotaging destinies on the bed of lustful pleasures, we miss out on our inheritance. Morality and character go together. If we are morally unstable like Reuben, we open ourselves up to sin. To partake our inheritance, we are to be in control of our flesh and its appetites and desires.

We must understand that dishonour is a wound that will most likely not heal without leaving a scar. We cannot dabble in sin and still expect to save our reputation, or expect to maintain a positive influence upon others. Though we know our sins were nailed to the cross, and that we are forever forgiven for past sins, we still have to suffer the consequences of some sins in our lives, which include remorse and a loss of reputation and influence. Others include illnesses, financial loss, incarceration and broken relationships.

It is important to point out that in spite of his action, God never disowned Reuben – he was still His child. You may have fallen – fallen badly, but our God is a God of restoration. The book of Revelation tells us that there will be 12,000 sealed from the tribe of Reuben who will be part of the messianic revival during the Great Tribulation. Therefore, we can say with confidence that if anyone is in Christ, the new creation has come; the old has gone, the new is here. (2 Corinthians 5:17).

Absalom

The story of Absalom can be summed up as one of a loving father and a rebellious son. Absalom was David's third son. The bible describes him as the most handsome man in the kingdom (2 Samuel 14:25). The story of Absalom is a sad story. It is sad for him, because he died in his sin, and that also should be a warning for us.

After Amnon, David's firstborn son, raped Absalom's sister Tamar, a terrible feud arose between the two half-brothers. Exceedingly vexed, Absalom's thirst for avenging his sister would only be quenched by Amnon's blood. Two years later, Absalom eventually managed to have his servants kill Amnon in cold blood, after which he fled to his maternal grandfather Talmai the king of Gershur and was a fugitive for three years.

Upon the intercession of Joab, Absalom safely returned home and was fully reinstated in his father's household. Unfortunately, when he came back home, Absalom developed a hatred for his father and designed a plot to dethrone him. He entrenched his influence and openly despised and opposed his father to the extent that David feared for his own life. He 'stole the hearts of the people of Israel' (2 Samuel 15) and eventually gained control of Hebron. He took over his father's house and slept with his concubines. This was considered an unforgivable and a greatly dishonourable act.

The aftermath of Absalom's rebellion against his father, was that he was eventually killed by his father's bodyguard during the Battle of Ephraim's Wood (2 Samuel 18).

The tragic reality is that Absalom's rebellion is being replayed over and over today in many people's lives, churches, families, organisations and in many nations as well. Absalom was a typical charismatic person and he managed to influence the people by stealing their hearts. But he was not the Lord's anointed. Nevertheless he was a prince and his inheritance would have been great. But he despised his father and wanted to dethrone him, the source of his inheritance.

What a big mistake. Even though he was handsome and his father was growing old, he had not right whatsoever to usurp his father's position.

It is hard to imagine the pain David suffered at the rebellion and dishonour of his own son. Ordinarily, it is a very difficult thing for anyone to face opposition and rebellion when in leadership. Can you imagine how much more it would hurt if the person who was doing it were your own flesh and blood, your own son? But David, like our heavenly father, could not stop loving Absalom and he mourned deeply for him after his was killed.

Rebellion is both hurtful and hurting. Rebellion against the ever-loving God hurts us in the process and where there is no repentance it leads to destruction. Dishonouring our heavenly father is one kind of a game we can never win. It may appear like we are winning for some time but in the long run there will be total loss. It is impossible to rebel and prosper.

From this story, we can clearly see the heart of God in David. It is David who pursued reconciliation, not

Absalom. It was the father's heart that yearned for his son. Absalom hurt his father, tried to ruin him and to kill him; but David loved him to the end. God's love is unconditional and no matter how rebellious we've been and no matter how bad we've treated him, he is always yearning for us to be reconciled back to him. David lost a son whom he loved. No matter what we do, God, our father, still loves us and has made all the provisions necessary for us to be saved. 'The Lord is not slack concerning His promise, as some count slackness, but is longsuffering toward us, not willing that any should perish but that all should come to repentance' (2 Peter. 3:9).

GROW TO MATURITY

> *"What I am saying is that as long as an heir is underage, he is no different from a slave, although he owns the whole estate. 2The heir is subject to guardians and trustees until the time set by his father."*
>
> *Galatians 4:1-2*

Through parables, Jesus did not just illustrate key Kingdom concepts but he also created meaning to His theology by reference to something more concrete. In Luke 15:11-32 Jesus tells a parable about a father and his two sons. Both come across as immature and not mindful of their inheritance.

To derive the authentic meaning of the parable, placing the same within its cultural context is pertinent. The best way of doing this is to place the parable in its original Jewish setting and then answer these two questions: How would first century Jews understand this illustration? What laws governed inheritance? The real gist of the story is the father and his relationship with his sons.

The younger son

The younger son has traditionally been referred to as 'the prodigal son'. The word *prodigal* comes from Latin: *prodigo* which means wasteful. This younger son did something that was utterly unthinkable and downright offensive if not illegal. He asked for his inheritance while his father was still alive and well, converted it into cash in a hurry, took the money and skipped town. He departed for a far away country where he squandered the money.

Kenneth Bailey, a respected New Testament scholar who spent over 15 years in the Middle East, asked all sorts of people in that part of the world, what it meant for a son to request his inheritance while his father was still alive and well. The answer was always the same: the son wanted his father dead! Only the father could initiate the process – not the heirs.

In his book, *The Cross and the Prodigal*, Kenneth further explains that if a Jewish son lost his inheritance among Gentiles, and then returned home, the community would perform a ceremony, called the *kezazah*. They would break a large pot in front of him and yell, "You are now cut off from your people!" The community would totally reject him.

One cannot help wondering what ran through the father's mind when his younger son asked for his inheritance before his death. In reality, the younger son wanted him dead. The audience must have gasped in shock and dismay as Jesus narrated the parable. The boy valued money more than his relationship with his father. He valued the blessings but had a blind spot on the source of the blessings. He wanted the supply but not a relationship with the source.

Many of us today are like the younger son. The younger son went to a far off country and wasted his inheritance. The idea portrayed in the story is that he goes as far away from his father as is humanly possible, like so many people who try to run away from their Father in heaven. They will travel to their own far away country and seek to be completely free from the loving care of their Creator. They want to live blessed lives but without God. They want their inheritance but reject a relationship with God. They desire to be free of the father. They want a form of godliness but deny the power therein.

Many of us disappear to far countries and live our lives as if God does not even exist. We waste our lives, our blessings, our talents and whatever good things the father has given us in riotous living, until that day when scarcity finds our address. About the time when the young man's money ran out, a great famine swept over the land and he began to starve. No one gave him anything. The young man became so hungry that even the pods he was feeding to the pigs looked good to him. The friends he was revelling with were nowhere to be seen. He was broke now and of no earthly use to them.

The renowned poem *The Second Coming* by Irish poet W. B. Yeats has a line that goes, *things fall apart when the centre cannot hold*. When our relationships compass fails to point to the true north, i.e. a relationship with God, no other relationship will last. When you sever your relationship with the true source of your blessings, down the line a time will come when you will be engulfed by an emptiness that cannot be filled by anything else. Any other relationship you seek will be because of a perceived advantage to you or to the other party. These relationships will vaporise when that perceived advantage is quenched.

Immature heirs suffer the risk of being prodigal with their inheritance. This is because they reason, think and speak as children. Immature heirs are self-centred and impatient. Self-centredness propels one to only look after their own interest, and what personal gain they get out of each and every relationship or project. This leads to greed, envy and unhealthy competition. Impatience makes people lose patience with God and with others include their vision enablers and destiny helpers. An impatient baby does not want to know if the milk is warming; they want it now and if not now, they want it five minutes ago!

Immature heirs do not cooperate with other people, have issues submitting to authority, always know who to blame and are unable to apologize when wrong. Consider the story of the Israelites in the wilderness. Poor Moses had to babysit hundreds of thousands of God's infants for a full generation.

The elder son

In the parable, Jesus in no uncertain terms says that the father actually divided his inheritance between both brothers (Luke 15:12). It is therefore not illogical to assume that the elder brother received his share of the inheritance alongside his younger brother. In fact, according to Jewish inheritance law, his share of the inheritance was twice as much as the younger brother's portion. In a sense, we can refer to the elder son as a prodigal son also. His younger brother was lost in the far country, but he was lost at home.

He (the elder son) did not step up and take responsibility and therefore his inheritance remained under the trusteeship of his father. He continued toiling and labouring like a slave for what was already his. The father maintained possession over the inheritance (Luke 15:22-24; 31). After the younger son came back home, the elder brother refused to join the joyous celebration. Consider his reaction: "Lo, these many years I have served you, and I never disobeyed your command! Yet you never gave me a young goat that I might throw a party with my friends! But when this son of yours came, who has devoured your living with harlots, you killed for him the fattened calf!"

(Luke 15:29-30). Jesus doesn't fault the morality, the obedience or the work ethic of this elder brother. However, He does fault his immature attitude as an heir.

Everything left in the house was legally his, including the butchered calf. The will had been probated and he had received his right to his inheritance. But we see his immaturity manifesting in the travesty of his identity in his father's house. It was one thing for the younger sibling wanting to be made a servant working hard to earn his keep, but it was entirely a different matter this elder son wasting time slaving, to earn blessings that were already rightfully his.

In the parable, the father reasoned with his son. " 'My son,' the father said, 'you are always with me, and everything I have is yours.' " (Luke 15:31). The father affirmed that the elder son is heir to everything the father possesses. Which was quite reassuring especially since the younger heir has already received and squandered his inheritance.

There are many people who claim to be mature in the Faith, yet they are still babies in so many ways. The Apostle Paul addressed this attitude in his epistles to the Corinthian church. The Corinthian Church that was endowed with much knowledge and many spiritual gifts. Yet, in spite of their many blessings and graces, they remained as babies in Christ. Here is his admonition: "Dear brothers and sisters, when I was with you I couldn't talk to you as I would to spiritual people. I had to talk as though you belonged to this world or as though you were infants in the Christian life. I had to feed you with milk, not with solid food, because you weren't ready for anything stronger. And you still aren't ready, for you are still controlled by your sinful nature. You are jealous of one another and quarrel with each other. Doesn't that prove you are controlled by your sinful nature? Aren't you living like people of the world?" (1 Corinthians 3: 1-3).

The older brother complained that his father did not even give him a young goat to feast with, much less a fattened calf. I'm sure the reason is not found in the father's stinginess, but that it didn't occur to the son to ask. James tells us, "You do not have, because you do not ask God. When you ask, you do not receive, because you ask with wrong motives, that you may spend what you get on your pleasures" (James 4:2-3).

The Bible says that as long as the heir is a child, he does not differ at all from a slave although he is owner of everything. His estate is under guardians and managers until the date set by the father. (Galatians 4: 1-2). They need someone mature to lead and guide them in the right direction. To partake of your inheritance, grow to maturity.

WALK IN DISCERNMENT

Of the sons of Issachar, men who understood the times, with knowledge of what Israel should do, their chiefs were two hundred; and all their kinsmen were at their command.

1 Chronicles 12:32

Mature Christians should be able to clearly discern good and evil (Hebrews 5:14). Discernment enables one to differentiate bctween that which is pleasing and provoking to God or that which is helpful or harmful to their souls.

Lack of discernment is what made Gehazi, the servant of Prophet Elisha, miss out on his inheritance. As the personal servant of Elisha, he was privileged to view mighty miracles that few people if any had seen. His name actually means *Valley of Vision*, yet he aborted the destiny that would have otherwise been his.

It was customary for the protégé of a great teacher or prophet, to prepare to step into office at the death of the master, as was the case between Elijah and Elisha. In Gehazi's case, he had the golden opportunity to grow in faith and in the office of the prophet. Gehazi had years to observe the way Elisha lived. His spiritual power and authority, his devotion to God, and his ministerial ethics and integrity. Gehazi was even entrusted with such a ministry as healing the sick and raising the dead, as in the case of the Shunamite woman's son. (2 Kings 4:29-31).

But in just one moment of unguarded lack of discernment, Gehazi blew it up in the account of the healing of Naaman the Syrian army commander, who had leprosy. Upon receiving complete healing of his disease, Naaman offered a huge reward to Elisha. Elisha refused the gift not willing to make merchandise of a gift of anointing from Yahweh. Rather than standing in awe of God's mighty healing power, Gehazi took it upon himself to follow after Naaman and request some silver and clothing, lying to Naaman that Elisha had sent him to receive the gift, on behalf of some young prophets who had just arrived and were in need.

There was a plethora of character flaws such as; greed, a lying spirit, disrespect for the prophet and lack of the fear of God. Upon returning to Elisha after accepting the gift and hiding it in his house, Gehazi attempted to lie but to no avail. He lacked discernment and also forgot that the Spirit of God revealed hidden things to

Elisha. When reprimanding him, Elisha rebuked his lack of discernment saying, "*Is this the time* to receive money and clothing, olive groves and vineyards, sheep and cattle, and male and female servants?" (2 Kings 5:26).

Elisha pronounced a curse of leprosy on Gehazi and all his future generations. His lack of discernment had cost him dearly. He forfeited his inheritance as a prophet, and aborted his destiny and legacy to his future generations. Gehazi performed not a single miracle, neither did he prophesy, in spite of being mentored by the prophet with the highest number of recorded miracles in the Bible (other than Jesus). Elisha took his anointing with him to the tomb. What a tragedy!

We need to mind our inheritance by walking in discernment and revelation. The Bile teaches that it is the responsibility of every child of God to be discerning. We are exhorted to examine everything carefully, to hold fast to that which is good and to abstain from every form of evil (1Thessalonians 5:21-

22). The Apostle Paul says, "I pray that the God of our Lord Jesus Christ, the Father of glory, may give unto you the spirit of wisdom and revelation in the knowledge of him," (Ephesians 1:17).

Discernment helps us to live an uncompromising life by ordering our thoughts, reasoning and conduct in accordance with the truth. Discernment enables us to measure the things we are taught against the immutable and infallible standard of God's Word.

We cannot understand our rich heritage using our cognitive perception; only by spiritual revelation. The carnal man does not perceive the things of the Spirit of God, for they are foolishness unto him; neither can he understand them because they are spiritually discerned (1 Corinthians 2:14). No eye has seen, no ear has heard, no heart has imagined what God has prepared for those who love Him. But God reveals all these to us by the Spirit. The Spirit searches all things, even the deep things of God and reveals them to us (2 Corinthians 2:9-10).

Discernment comes to us through God's Word and through revelation by the power of the Holy Spirit. We do not get discernment because we saw, heard, smelt, tasted, or touched something. Jesus said that it was not flesh and blood that revealed to Peter that Jesus was the Christ and the Son of the Living God. He did not discern who Jesus was through seeing, touching, hearing, tasting, or smelling. It was revealed to him from the Father in heaven.

God does not want us to be ignorant about Him, His counsel or His purpose. The Bible says, "Surely the Lord GOD does nothing unless He reveals His secret counsel To His servants the prophets," (Amos 3:7). It is incumbent upon us, therefore, to spend time with God in prayer, soaking in His word and yielding to the Holy Spirit.

TAKING IT BY FORCE

> *"See I have set the land before you. Go in and POSSESS the Land which the Lord swore to give you."*
>
> *Deuteronomy 1:8*

There is a popular Latin that says, '*praemonitus, praemunitus*'. Loosely translated, this means 'forewarned is forearmed'. The scriptures firmly remind us on the dangers of being ignorant. Being ignorant sends God's people to the grave (Job 36:12), sends them to exile (Isaiah 5:13) and makes them perish (Hosea 4:6).

In order to possess our inheritance, we must first know of its existence. We must be fully persuaded that God's promises belong to us. Now all the promised blessings of God are already paid for by the blood of Christ and so are free to us, but we still have to lay hold of them and make them ours (Ephesians 3:12). Knowing about it is not enough; in order to enjoy it we must possess it. I may know the promise of God is true, but I must receive it so that it is true for me.

Jesus in His gospel, called people to repentance saying, "The Kingdom of God is at hand" (Matthew 4:17). *At hand* means it is here; it is within reach. The Kingdom of God with all its blessings, including salvation, is at hand. God is holding out to us the blessing as a free-gift, for us to come to Him and reach out with our hand of faith and lay hold of it. This is the Gospel Jesus told us to preach. "Preach: "the Kingdom of Heaven is at hand" (Matthew 10:7). The Gospel is the proclamation that He offers us His Life, so that it is freely available to us to reach out and receive. The inheritance is yours for the taking, it is at hand, so reach out and take it.

Once the Israelites became persuaded that the Promised Land was theirs to possess, they pressed in and took it. Jesus said that from the days of John the Baptist until now the Kingdom of Heaven suffers violence, and the violent take it by force (Matthew 11:12). We are to forcefully lay hold of the inheritance that God has already provided for us. He has put it at hand, within our reach, for us to come to Him and receive, having been purchased by His Blood.

But we must remember that Satan is intent on fighting us every inch of the way, as we pursue our inheritance. Just as God has a plan for our lives, so does the devil who will endeavour to use wiles and schemes to try and take our inheritance from us (John 10:10). God has given us the authority and power to send the devil running, and He has also told us how to do it. We must know how to recognise and deal with him, and be ready to resist him when he comes to challenge, deny and steal the Word from our heart (and thus steal the blessing from our life).

This means there's a battle for your inheritance! Entering and possessing your 'Promised Land' means you must be willing to engage the enemy. We therefore cannot afford to be ignorant of the enemy's schemes when waging war against him (2 Corinthians 2:11). King Solomon, the wisest man ever, admonishes us that it is not wise to go charging into battle without a plan (Pro 20:18).

The Battle Belongs to the Lord

We are called to take our position and see the Lord valiantly fight for us. Take a position of faith. Be convinced the battle is the Lord's. Any demon that comes against you has to come against Christ in you.

Position yourself in prayer and take on the spiritual armour.

"This is what the Lord says to you: 'Do not be afraid or discouraged because of this vast army. For the battle is not yours, but God's. Tomorrow march down against them. They will be climbing up by the Pass of Ziz, and you will find them at the end of the gorge in the Desert of Jeruel. You will not have to fight this battle. Take up your positions; stand firm and see the deliverance the Lord will give you, Judah and Jerusalem. Do not be afraid; do not be discouraged. Go out to face them tomorrow, and the Lord will be with you.'" (2 Chronicles 20: 15-17).

After taking your position, you need to stand firm. Stand still and await God's mighty deliverance. "Fear not, stand firm, and see the salvation of the Lord, which he will work for you today; for the Egyptians whom you see today, you shall never see again. The Lord will fight for you, and you have only to be still." (Exodus. 14:13-14)

After Moses saw the victory of the Lord, He stopped complaining about his enemy's activity and celebrated the deliverance of God. He sang a song and said "the LORD is a man of war; the LORD is his name." Exodus 15:3.

Standing still means not wavering as you rest assured that God is handling and perfecting all that which concerns you. Stop feeling as though you need to take matters into your own hands. Do not try to 'help' God by devising human schemes of winning the battle. Stop all your efforts to deliver yourself. Acknowledge that God alone can save you. "Be still, and know that I am God: I will be exalted among the heathen, I will be exalted in the earth." Psalm 46:10.

The Battle belongs to the lord. It is the Lord's battle to fight – not yours. "And I commanded Joshua at that time, 'Your eyes have seen all that the LORD your God has done to these two kings. *So will the LORD do* to all the kingdoms into which you are crossing." (Deuteronomy 3:21).

"Be strong and courageous. Do not be afraid or dismayed before the king of Assyria and the entire horde that is with him, for there are more with us than with him. With him is an arm of flesh, but *with us is the LORD our God, to help us and to fight our battles.*" (2 Chronicles 32:7-8

"For thus says the LORD, 'Even the captives of the mighty shall be taken, and the prey of the tyrant be rescued, for *I will contend with those who contend with you,* and I will save your children.'" (Isaiah 49:25).

The full armour of God

It is widely accepted that the main theme of Ephesians is the church, which is the body of Christ. Most theologians regard *Ephesians* to be a circular letter intended for many churches. It was written from Rome during Paul's first imprisonment, and the armour seems to be in direct correlation with that of the Roman Empire's soldiers.

Later on, having been imprisoned by the emperor Nero, Paul wrote to encourage the young pastor Timothy in Ephesus. Timothy was facing severe conflicts in his ministry at Ephesus, and the relentless opposition from heretics, apostates, and persecutors was weakening him.

Just like any Christian who experiences difficulty because of following Christ, Timothy needed to be reminded again of his task— to endure hardship as a good soldier of Jesus Christ. Paul encouraged and challenged him to endure with him, like a good soldier of Christ Jesus (2 Timothy 2:3).

As soldiers in the army of the Lord, that is what we are called to do. Paul's words to Timothy are your marching orders too; therefore, you need to strive to be a good soldier of Christ Jesus. You need to put on the full armour of God.

The full armour of God helps us to stand against the *schemes* of the devil. The Greek word translated *schemes* is *methodia*, which gives us the English word method. It refers to craftiness, cunningness, and deception.

We have to put on the full armour of God, so that when the day of evil comes, we may be able to stand our ground. The day of evil will surely come. Paul says, '*When,* not *if,* the day of evil comes because nothing is more certain than the conflict in the heavenly realm.

The armour of God also helps us to hold our ground after the battle. Four times in Ephesians 6:10-14, Paul urges us to stand firm in the battle against the devil's schemes. Paul ends this clarion call by exhorting us to pray fervently for ourselves, for each other and for the work of the Church.

Trust God

Trust isn't an easy thing to come by, yet it is one of the most important parts of our relationship with God. When times are tough and things aren't going our way, that's when we find it the most difficult to trust God.

We doubt that God is going to come through for us, we lack faith in His promises, and we worry ourselves with endless thoughts about our future. The problem is, this is the exact opposite of how God wants us to react to the difficult circumstances in our lives.

God wants us to trust Him when we're having doubts and are unsure about what to do. He wants us to believe in His promises when we think that things are going to get worse. To trust is not just to believe that God is able; it is to depend upon him and submit to Him as He does it.

The amazing story of Charles Blondin, a famous French tightrope walker, is a wonderful illustration of what trust is. Blondin's greatest fame came on September 14, 1860, when he became the first person to cross a tightrope stretched 11,000 feet (over a quarter of a mile) across the mighty Niagara Falls. People from both Canada and America came from miles away to see this great feat. He walked across, 160 feet above the falls, several times... each time with a different daring feat - once in a sack, on stilts, on a bicycle, in the dark, and blindfolded.

One time he even carried a stove and cooked an omelette in the middle of the rope! A large crowd gathered and the buzz of excitement ran along both sides of the river bank, as Blondin carefully walked across - one dangerous step after another - pushing a wheelbarrow holding a sack of potatoes. The crowd's applause was louder than the roar of the falls!

Then at one point, he decided to ask for the participation of a volunteer. Upon reaching the other side, Blondin suddenly stopped and addressed his audience: "Do you believe I can carry a person across in this wheelbarrow?" The crowd enthusiastically yelled, "Yes! You are the greatest tightrope walker in the world. We believe!" "Okay," said Blondin, "Who wants to get into the wheelbarrow." As far as the Blondin story goes, no one did at the time!

This unique story illustrates a real life picture of what trust actually is. The crowd watched these daring feats. They said they believed. But their response proved they truly did not trust him. Similarly, it is one thing for us to say we believe in God. However, it's true trust when we believe God and put our faith and trust in His Son, Jesus Christ.

Proverb 3:5-7 gives a blue print for trusting God: "Trust in the Lord with all your heart and do not lean on your own understanding. In all your ways acknowledge Him, and He will make your paths straight. Do not be wise in your own eyes; Fear the Lord and turn away from evil."

Set your heart on God. Not in a creature, not in a man: but on the Lord, the object of all grace, and in him only. "Cursed are those who put their trust in mere humans, who rely on human strength and turn their hearts away from the LORD." (Jeremiah 7:5)

Do not lean on your understanding. Not on riches, strength, and wisdom, education etc. "What sorrow awaits those who look to Egypt for help, trusting their horses, chariots, and charioteers and depending on the strength of human armies instead of looking to the Lord, the Holy One of Israel." (Isaiah 31:1).

Do not be wise in your own eyes. Do not be crafty; do not sin to make it happen then say "God blessed me". The Bible says that the wisdom of this world is foolishness to God (1 Corinthians 3:19) and that God traps the wise in the snare of their own cleverness so their cunning schemes are thwarted (Job 5:13). The wisdom of those who are wise in their own eyes is worthless (Psalms 94:11). Whatever we think we know, the Lord knows more.

In all your ways acknowledge God. The more you know God, the easier it is to trust him. This doesn't just mean intellectual awareness, but an act of perceiving God's character and will in every moment of life. The more you acknowledge the power of God in your daily walk with Him, the easier it becomes to trust him for what lies ahead

"Blessed are those who trust in the LORD and have made the LORD their hope and confidence. He is like a tree planted by water, that sends out its roots by the stream, and does not fear when heat comes, for its leaves remain green, and is not anxious in the year of drought, for it does not cease to bear fruit." (Jeremiah 17:7-8)

"May the God of hope fill you with all joy and peace as you trust in him, so that you may overflow with hope by the power of the Holy Spirit." Romans 15:13 (NIV).

ASK FOR THE NATIONS

"I will surely tell of the decree of the LORD: He said to me, 'You are My Son, today I have begotten you. Ask of me, and I will surely give the nations as your inheritance, and the very ends of the earth as your possession'"

(Psalms 2:7-8).

Why is it, that some parts of the world seem to be experiencing an open heaven characterised by undeniable outpouring of the power of God, while other parts appear to be experiencing a spiritual drought? Evangelistic campaigns in various places in Africa and Asia are experiencing thousands and thousands of people being saved, delivered and healed in a single meeting, yet other parts like Western Europe nothing much seems to be happening?

God can withhold rain from some people yet release a mighty outpouring to others. Amos 4:7 says God "would send rain on one city, on another city he would withhold the rain. One piece of ground would be rained on, while the part not rained on would dry up. The city without rain would have no harvest." In other words, NO RAIN NO HARVEST.

Rain represents the outpouring of the Holy Spirit and an open heaven. This is what Prophet Isaiah prophesied: "I will pour out water on the thirsty land and streams on the dry ground, I will pour out my

Spirit on your offspring, and My blessing on your descendants." (Isaiah 44:3).

Rain means life, recovery, restoration, the rivers will run again, fish will be caught again, the crops will grow again, there will be joy where there has been sorrow, there will be laughter where there has been weeping.

The early rain revived the parched and thirsty soil and prepared it for the seed. The latter rain came before the harvest and contributed to maturation and ripening of the crop. These seasons ensured that God's people gather in the grain, the wine and the oil. These three represent spiritual nourishment, revival and refreshment and the anointing.

God has promised to give us rain – outpouring of the Holy Spirit – in the right seasons. "He will give the rain for your land in its season, the early rain and the later rain, that you may gather in your grain and your wine and your oil," (Deut 11:14).

The Scriptures exhort us to pray for an outpouring "Ask rain from the Lord at the time of the latter rain. The Lord who makes the clouds will give you showers of rain and vegetation in the field to each man," Zechariah 10:1.

God spoke to King Solomon after he dedicated the temple and openly declared there will be times when He may have to "shut the heavens and withhold the rain" as a form of judgement. In so doing, He intends to turn the heart of His people back to Him wherein they humble themselves, pray, seek his presence and turn their backs on their wicked ways. Only then will God heal the land. (2Chr. 7:13-14).

One of the reasons why God holds back the rain (outpouring/open heavens) is when the church allows the spirit of Ahab to operate. Ahab is said to have done more evil than the kings before him. He married Jezebel, the daughter of the king of Tyre and Sidon (I Kings 16:30-31). This was in spite of admonitions of God that the Israelites should not intermarry with idol worshipers (Deuteronomy 7:1, 3-4).

Ahab's spirit operating in the church hinders the people of God from experiencing an outpouring and open heavens. God indicts His people through Prophet Micah decreeing that as a result of following the example of wicked King Ahab, they will have no harvest; no grain, no oil and no wine. (Micah 6:15-16).

Ahab lived in Jezreel, which means a place of revelation, yet he walked in darkness. A man with Ahab's spirit may believe there is a God, but it is just not worth the effort or time it takes to commit his life to Him.

Ahab is devoted to everything that God hates and forbids. Ahab replaces Jehovah with idols of Baal and Asherah. Apostle Paul equates idol worship to demonic worship (1 Corinthians 10:20). Baal worship was rooted in sensuality and involved ritualistic prostitution in the temples. At times, appeasing Baal required human sacrifice.

Ahab is the permissive spirit that allows Jezebel to go wild and out of control. We talk a lot about Jezebel, but this wicked principality relies on Ahab to maximize its authority and propagate its immorality and idolatry. He is the authority figure that she gets her INITIAL authority from. To completely remove Jezebel, you have to remove Ahab first.

To bring back the rain, we need Elijah to rise and confront Ahab. Elijah's mandate was to deal with Ahab's apostasy and restore the worship of Jehovah. His name means: Jehovah is my God. Elijah was sent to confront not comfort. He confronted the man who had opened a floodgate of wickedness and in so doing made shut the heavens.

For us to experience an open heaven we have to stop pampering and mollycoddling sin. Confront! You cannot subdue without confronting. "From the days of John the Baptist until now the kingdom of heaven suffers violence, and the violent take it by force," (Matthew 11:12). John the Baptist came in the spirit of Elijah. Elijah carried a revival kind of a spirit – a conquering attitude and determination to battle against idol worship.

To confront the spirit of Ahab, we need to arise and take our rightful position. Our rightful position is one of authority wielded through righteousness and fervent praying. Elijah walked into the presence of idol-worshipping King and shut the heavens in his face.

Baal was the God of rain and harvest and generally fertility. Baal idol was in a shape of a bull representing fertility and lust for power and sexual pleasure. But the authority of God's Word spoken by the prophet paralysed the idol for three years. "Elijah was a man just like us. He prayed earnestly that it would not rain, and it did not rain on the land for three and a half years. Again he prayed, and the heavens gave rain, and the earth yielded its crops." (James 5:17-18).

Elijah was a man of faith. When he told Ahab that there was "a sound of abundance of rain," (1 King 18:41), there had as yet been no sound audible to the human ear. When the servant SAW a small cloud, Elijah HEARD a sound of the roar of a heavy shower. What a faith. Martin Luther said, "Faith sees the invisible, believes the incredible and receives the impossible."

It takes faith to bring revival. Faith is the substance of things hoped for, the evidence of things not seen. It takes faith to stand before Pharaoh and say "Let my people go!" It takes faith to stand before Goliath and say "You come against me with sword, spear, and javelin, but I come against you in the name of the LORD Almighty."

Faith is the absolute conviction that God will always do what He has promised. Faith pertains to the things that we cannot perceive by our natural senses 'for we live by faith, not by sight.' (2 Corinthians 5:7). Natural senses produce a conviction or evidence of visible or tangible things; faith is the spiritual sense, which enables us to see the invisible realm. Faith is the assurance, the confidence and the conviction of the reality of things hoped for. Faith is the evidence, the proof and the certainty that what we cannot see exists. (Hebrews 11:1).

The call to live by faith is a call to rise above facts and realities of life. Facts do not diminish or lessen the power of God. Living by faith means going beyond reason or any fact that is not in line with the word of God and simply taking God at His word, however illogical and senseless it might appear. In our humanity, some things seem so impossible that we cannot think of them as possibilities. 'But with God all things are possible.' (Matt 19:26).

Faith sees the invisible and believes the impossible. Faith calls the things that are not as though they are. For example, it takes faith for one to boldly declare, 'next year at this time you will be holding a son in your arms!' (2 Kings 4:16). Faith rejoices without seeing or understanding what God is doing. When we fail to operate by faith, we limit the work of God in our lives. This is because without faith it is impossible to please God, (Heb 11:6).

Faith pertains to things that we hope for. Hope is a confident expectation. We hope for things that we cannot see with our natural eyes. 'Hope that is seen is no hope at all. Who hopes for what they already have?' (Romans 8:24). If you have the substance before you, if you can see it, what use is there for faith? Faith is needed for that which we can't see and can't touch.

Faith is the confidence that hope will be fulfilled. The things we hope for must be based on the word of God and not just carnal desires. Faith is having full confidence in reality of God's promises, purpose and will upon our lives. Faith is predicated on judging that God is faithful and able to keep His promises (Hebrews 11:11). By doing so, Sarah received strength to conceive seed. God gave the strength, but Sarah had to receive it by faith.

God longs for His people to arise and bring about a change instead of cowering in fear. "You shall declare a thing and the Lord will establish it for you," *(Job 22:28).* And who knows whether you have not come to the kingdom (family, office, school, church, city, country) for such a time as this?" (Esther 4:14).

We will bring back revival. "'Not by might nor by power, but by my Spirit', says the LORD Almighty". (Zechariah 4:6). For we "can do all things through Christ who strengthens us." (Phil 4:13).

Winds of revival in India

A short-term mission trip is an intense experience in many ways. During summer of 2015, I had a once in a lifetime opportunity to minister in India. My friend, brother and partner in ministry, Rev David Gitogo Githiga (Senior Pastor Nairobi Christian Centre – Kenya), accompanied me. He likes being called Pastor GG. We went to there with a prayer in our hearts that we would be fruitful ministers of the Gospel. We had a burning desire that the lives of the people we were to minister to, would be transformed more into the likeness of Jesus. We desired and prayed that our message and our preaching would not be with wise and persuasive words, but with a demonstration of the Spirit's power (1 Corinthians 2:4).

By God's grace we were able to reach out to hundreds of people from Banzara tribal community in Repudi Thanda, Krishna District under the invitation of Banzara Tribal Ministries (BTM). We went to India covered in the prayers of our family, friends, intercessory teams and the Church. I can confidently report that God answered all those prayers in a mighty way!

Before the trip I had much anticipation about what God wanted to accomplish through us. I flew from London Heathrow airport and when I linked up with Pastor GG at Rajiv Gandhi International Airport in Hyderabad, I realized that he had the same enthusiasm and I knew for sure that we were going to impact Repudi Thanda with the Gospel. We didn't know what was ahead but we knew what to expect. Miracles, signs and wonders! We knew God had not only sent us, but that He had gone ahead of us and was actually with us.

Upon arrival, we were humbled by the love, sincerity and warmth of the Banzara tribal people. They may not have much in the way of material wealth by most standards, but the joy and passion that many of them have because of Christ, reminded me that Jesus is all that you need.

The Banzara tribal community was very happy to see us arrive after many months of preparation and anticipation. We had opportunities to visit with the village people and we did intensive one-to-one ministry.

There were many memorable moments. I am eternally grateful to God for the opportunity he gave us to be used of Him. Salvation decisions were recorded – these were mainly conversions from Hinduism to Christianity. We witnessed miracles, healings and deliverance. There was a manifest apostolic and prophetic grace during the mission trip. The gospel was powerfully proclaimed and well received. We also showed the Jesus Film for two nights and almost everyone who came to watch came forward to accept Jesus at the end of the show.

We spent quality time ministering to BTM Pastors from all over A. Konduru Mandal. We encouraged them to continue serving God amidst the persecutions and other challenges for their labour is not in vain.

Every day, we visited the children and orphans being cared for by BTM. The children there are so precious. We taught them about Jesus, played games and taught them a few songs about Jesus. We also prayed for them.

We went for home-to-home ministry every day. We prayed for many sick people. The miracle worker, Jesus Christ healed those who were sick. The glory of God was manifest throughout and we declared the Gospel under a heavy unction.

One 16 year old girl, Lakshmi, who was dumb since she was a child was totally set free after we cast out the dumb spirit oppressing her. She beamed with the joy after being set free. She cried tears of joy and we couldn't help crying with her. She went home saying the Name of Jesus, which she couldn't do before. It was glorious.

As I watched the faces of the children and the adults when we told them about Jesus and after they received their miracles, I knew that God had truly sent us there. We prayed together, cried together and we hugged one another with a Christian love that I cannot explain.

During our first meeting, we prayed for a dumb boy named Prabhas Bhukya. God touched him instantly, loosed his tongue and gave him speech. We laid hands on him and prophetically declared in the name of Jesus that he will become a great preacher in India. The following day, we went to the boy's home and we learnt that his dad, Lalyu Bhukya, was admitted at Vijayawada hospital with multiple organ failure. The boy's uncle told us that when the man was being admitted, his liver and kidney had failed and that he was bleeding from the nose and the mouth. We prayed for Lalyu and stood on Psalms 107:20. That very moment, Jehovah Rapha showed up at the hospital bed where Lalyu was admitted and healed him immediately. Later that evening he was discharged and went home. All the glory to God! We serve a miracle working God.

Testimonies of what God did almost one year ago have not ceased. Here is Kalyani's Testimony. Kalyani is a niece to our host Rev John Banavadhu.

Kalyani and her husband had waited for a baby for 7yrs. She travelled to the meeting but the husband was left at home attending to other matters. They had given up on doctors but not on God. Her story changed during the last night meeting when she requested us to pray for her. We prayed for her and prophesied that she would conceive and have a healthy baby, so audacious was our faith that I told her that the next time I ever set foot in India I will go and play with the baby that we had prayed for. Pastor GG asked her to name her baby and start nesting and preparing for the baby. She activated her faith and said that if God gives her a boy his name shall be Victor.

Few months later, during Christmas, Rev Banavadhu's son, Stephen, (Kalyani's cousin) notified Both Pastor GG and I, that Kalyani had conceived and was faring well with her pregnancy. In July 2016, God blessed Kalyani and her husband with a bouncing baby girl! With God, all things are possible.

Miracles still happen. Do not give up hope. There's nothing too hard for God. At the appointed time, may God deal with you graciously. Even as you read this, receive your miracle in the name of Jesus.

I urge you to continue praying for the church in India. The church in India is currently going through a difficult phase but I thank God because He is leading them in triumph in Christ. (2 Corinthians 2:14). They are waling under an open heaven in the midst of persecutions and other social-cultural challenges. The Lord is adding daily to those who are being saved, and miracles signs and wonders are testifying powerfully to the power of the resurrected Christ.

RE-DIGGING THE WELLS OF REVIVAL

"LORD, you poured out blessings on your land! You restored the fortunes of Israel. You forgave the guilt of your people, yes, you covered all their sins. You held back your fury. You kept back your blazing anger. Now restore us again, O God of our salvation. Put aside your anger against us once more. Will you be angry with us always? Will you prolong your wrath to all generations? Won't you revive us again, so your people can rejoice in you? Show us your unfailing love, O LORD, and grant us your salvation."

Psalms 85:1-7

God indicted His people, through prophet Jeremiah, for abandoning pure water from the living well and hewing cisterns to collect surface water. "'Be appalled at this, you heavens, and shudder with great horror,' declares the Lord. 'My people have committed two sins: They have forsaken me, the spring of living water, and have dug their own cisterns, broken cisterns that cannot hold water.'" Jeremiah 2:23

Their first evil was desertion of God. They had forsaken the fountain of living waters in whom they had an abundant and constant supply of unquenchable supply of living water.

Their second evil was attempting to find a substitute. They took a great deal of pain to hew cisterns. They dug pits or pools which they would carry water to, and which would receive the surface water.

But these cisterns proved to be broken cisterns, false at the bottom, so that they could hold no water. When they came to quench their thirst there they found nothing but mud and mire, and the filthy sediments of a standing pool. In actual fact God further indicted them for backsliding, which he likened to Egypt to drink water from the Nile and going to Assyria to drink water from the Euphrates. (Jeremiah 2:18)

A cistern is designed to store water, not to tap an existing water source. Cisterns usually collect surface water, which is exposed, to many different contaminants, such as animal waste, pesticides, insecticides, industrial waste, and many other organic materials in addition to dead and decaying matter.

Very typical, to mans nature. When man departs from God, he precipitates himself on a variety of objects and devotes himself to a variety of pursuits with the view of indemnifying himself.

In Genesis 26, we read that Isaac recognized his hereditary right and responsibility to re-dig and restore the ancient wells of his father Abraham, which the Philistines stopped up after he died. It was after re-digging his father's wells that the Lord appeared to Isaac and pronounced over him the same blessing previously spoken over Abraham. Not long after that, the Lord allowed Isaac to unearth his very own well.

It is paramount to note that the location where Abraham dug the wells was not the Promised Land. He was still a sojourner in the land of the Philistines at a place known as Gerar. Gerar belonged to the Philistines.

Years later, Isaac found himself in a situation identical to the one in which his father had been and did exactly as his father. God blessed him too and "he had so many flocks and herds and servants that the Philistines envied him. So all the wells that his father's servants had dug in the time of his father Abraham, the Philistines stopped filling them with earth." (Genesis 26:14)

After Isaac was told to move away by Abimelech, he set up tents and settled down at the Valley of Gerar. By this time, he was already a very wealthy man. He then reopened the wells his father had dug, which the Philistines had filled in after Abraham's death. Isaac also restored the names Abraham had given them. (Genesis 26:18).

But then the shepherds from Gerar came and claimed the well. "This is our water," they said, and they argued over it with Isaac's herdsmen. So Isaac named the well Esek (which means "argument"). Isaac's men then dug another well, but again there was a dispute over it. So Isaac named it Sitnah (which means "hostility"). (Genesis 26: 20-21).

The Philistines covered up the wells because Abraham was dead and also because they envied Isaac. They filled the wells with dirt but when they were undug, the wells were still flowing with fresh water. The Philistines then disputed over the ownership of the wells. This was in spite of the fact that Abraham had already paid the price to Abimelech the King of Gerar. (Genesis 21).

More often than not, revivals are usually beset by controversies swirling around miracles and manifestations, excesses, suspicions, scandals, and a myriad of theological disputes. However, there is no need to dispute over the work of God. There is actually no time to waste fighting over dogmas and non-issues whilst millions are still dying and slipping to a Christ-less eternity. "It is true that some preach Christ out of envy and rivalry, but others out of goodwill. The latter do so out of love, knowing that I am put here for the defence of the gospel. The former preach Christ out of selfish ambition, not sincerely, supposing that they can stir up trouble for me while I am in chains. But what does it matter? The important thing is that in every way, whether from false motives or truth, Christ is preached. And because of this I rejoice. Yes, and I will continue to rejoice." (Philippians 1:15-18).

The thirst for fresh water pushed Isaac beyond the jealousy, disputes and hostility levied on him. Do not let your hunger and thirst for revival, for a true authentic move of God be stopped by disparagers, sceptics and pessimists. He kept on digging and rose above the opposition. Do not let unfair treatment inhibit you or hinder you in the pursuit of your purpose.

As a seed of Abraham, Isaac was inherently blessed and empowered to prosper no matter what the enemy tried.

After Isaac moved away, Abimelech came to him one day and testified, "We have certainly seen that the Lord is with you… and now look how the Lord has blessed you!" (Gen 26:28-29).

He relocated and continued digging and God gave him room to flourish. This time round, Isaac gave the new wells new names. He stopped relying on the revelation of his father and encountered God for himself. He raised an altar and worshipped God, and God renewed His covenant.

Conferring names is a sign of authority. Thus, you need to be vigilant the names you confer. Because whatever you call something or someone, so they become. This was the first authority that Adam exercised at the Garden of Eden. "And out of the ground the LORD God formed every beast of the field, and every fowl of the air; and brought them to Adam to see what he would call them: and whatever Adam called every living creature, that was the name thereof." (Genesis 2:19).

God gives names as well. Even more significant is when He changes a name. When God changes a name, it indicates that something new has happened or will happen to that person—a new relationship, a new character quality, or a new phase of life.

Isaac giving new names to the wells teaches us a very important lesson. We cannot fit a new move of God in an old outfit. We need new wineskins for new wine. We have a rich heritage, but the essence of the new covenant, is that every person may know God for themselves. To each new generation under a new dispensation, God reveals himself afresh and renews his covenant.

Revivals and awakenings a road well-travelled. From powerful revivals of the eighteenth century that spread through Europe, especially England and North America; to revival movements of the last decade of the twentieth century leading into the twenty first century. The latter characterised by huge healing evangelism crusades and mega-churches such as Yoido Full Gospel Church in Korea numbering a million by 2010. Each revival or awakening leaves its own signature, yet all share a common theme: the transforming presence of God.

MIND THE PRESENCE OF GOD.

"You will show me the path of life; In Your presence is fullness of joy; At Your right hand are pleasures forevermore."

Psalms 16:11

In order for us to move forward in fulfilling God's purposes for our generation, we must reach back to remember, honour and add to what He has done, through previous generations through His presence. When we tap once more into HIS presence we will experience a release, a fresh river of His glory to flow into our generation.

The presence of God is not simply just an aura or atmosphere, but an aspect of the nature of God. It's good for a church to be growing, to have an electric atmosphere, to have great worship, and to have exciting meetings. But far more important than all of those things is the answer to this question: Are we experiencing God's transforming presence?

The presence of God dwells in a Sanctuary. God instructed the children of Israel to make a dwelling place for His habitation. "Let them make Me a sanctuary, that I may dwell among them." Exodus 25:8.

The Bible begins and ends with the presence of God. In Genesis Eden is presented as Man's home, but more importantly as God's sanctuary, i.e. a dwelling place for His presence. In Revelation, We see Eden returning and being expanded into a New Heaven and a New Earth where God's people enjoy God's presence continually. (Rev 21:14).

We also see in the Sinai Covenant, that at the heart of it was the promise that God's presence would dwell with His People. "Then I will dwell among the Israelites and be their God. They will know that I am the Lord their God, who brought them out of Egypt so that I might dwell among them. I am the Lord their God." (Exodus 29: 45 – 46).

In the account of Samson, the last judge of Israel before introduction of monarchies (Judges 13 to 16), we see his destiny explicitly being laid out by God even before he was born. Samson was given immense strength to aid him against his enemies and allow him to perform glorious exploits, such as killing a lion, slaying an entire army of one thousand Philistines with only the jawbone of a donkey, gathering three hundred foxes, and using them to torch the grain fields and olive groves of the Philistines, and destroying a temple of the Philistines with his bare hands and many other exploits.

When a child was given especially to God, or when a man gave himself to work for God, he was forbidden to drink wine, and as a sign, his hair was left to grow long while the vow or promise to God was upon him. Such a person as this was called a Nazarite, a word which means "one who has a vow"; and Samson was to be a Nazarite, and under a vow, as long as he lived.

In spite of his continued directive from God to fight the Philistines, Samson pursued a much more personal connection with them. He fell in love with a Philistine woman, Delilah, who was tasked by her people to find the secret of Samson's strength. Three times she begged to know the secret of his strength, and three times he lied to her. Finally, after Delilah nagged persistently, he confessed: "A razor has never come to my head; for I have been a Nazirite to God from my mother's womb. If my head were shaved, then my strength would leave me" (Judges 16:17). God supplied Samson's power because of his consecration to God as a Nazirite, symbolized by the fact that a razor had never touched his head.

Sure enough, Delilah took advantage of this new information, lulling Samson to sleep and shaving off his hair. He immediately became weak and God's power left him. "Samson woke up and thought, 'I will do as I did before and shake myself free.' but he did not realise that the Lord had left him." (Judges 16:20). What a horrible tragedy not to KNOW that God is not with you. His long hair had been cut off, the vow to the Lord was broken, and the Lord had left him. He was now as weak as other men, and helpless in the hands of his enemies. Delilah handed Samson over to the Philistines, who gouged out his eyes, and forced him work grinding grain by turning a large millstone in prison.

We can no longer afford to take God's grace for granted. We cannot keep on abusing the mercies of God and keep on doing what we want and expect that God will still have our back. It is a sad thing for anyone or for a nation, to end up in a place where God's hand is no longer on them. But it is more tragic to think that His hand is still on them when in actual fact it is not.

When Saul was anointed as King, the Bible records that the Spirit of God rushed to him (1 Sam 10:10). However, when he messed with the anointing, the Bible says that the Spirit of God departed from him (1 Sam 16:14). The tragedy was; he continued reigning as king for 15 more years after God withdrew His spirit.

Do not deceive yourself that God is still with you. Either, because you are not reaping immediate consequences of your reprobation, or you appear to be walking from blessing to blessing. The biggest forms of deception we are facing today are: the lies we tell ourselves, the facts we have chosen to ignore, the truth we have closed our ears to and the realities we have shut our eyes to... Lord have mercy on us! "Cast me not away from your presence, and take not your Holy Spirit from me." (Ps 51:11).

The presence of God was the distinguishing factor in the life of Joseph as well. "The LORD was with Joseph, and he was a prosperous man; and he was in the house of his master the Egyptian. And his master saw that the LORD was with him, and that the LORD made all that he did, to prosper in his hand. Joseph found grace in his sight, and he served him: and he made him overseer his house, and all that he had, he put into his hand. And it came to pass from the time that he had made him overseer his house, and over all that he had, that the LORD blessed the Egyptian's house for Joseph's sake; and the blessing of the LORD was on all that he had in the house, and in the field." (Gen 28: 2- 5)

Just like Moses at the burning bush, God wants us to go beyond being awed by signs, miracles and wonders, to being discerning of His divine Presence. God's presence begets signs miracles and wonders. If you don't discern HIS presence, watch out because you could be staring at a strange fire! It is all about the holy ground and not just the burning bush.

Mind the presence of God. For you to lay hold of, and possess your inheritance, you need to abide in the presence of God.

LET THE WEAK SAY I AM STRONG

"Even though I have received such wonderful revelations from God. So to keep me from becoming proud, I was given a thorn in my flesh, a messenger from Satan to torment me and keep me from becoming proud. Three different times I begged the Lord to take it away. Each time he said, 'My grace is all you need. My power works best in weakness.' So now I am glad to boast about my weaknesses, so that the power of Christ can work through me. That's why I take pleasure in my weaknesses, and in the insults, hardships, persecutions, and troubles that I suffer for Christ. For when I am weak, then I am strong."

2 Corinthians 12:7 – 10

Weaknesses are those circumstances, situations or wounds that make us look weak; things we would probably get rid of if we had the human strength. We all have our afflictions and weaknesses, that we strive to change and overcome.

We have weaknesses mainly to keep us humble, and so that God may be glorified by showing himself strong on our behalf. It is important to bear in mind that though we are not of this world, we are still in this world. Time and time again situations will remind us that we have not yet gone to heaven and that we are still mastering a human experience here on earth.

I have been a pastor for a while now, and it has been long enough to know that we've got weak people in the church. Good born again brothers and sisters who are water baptised, Holy Ghost filled and tongue-speaking, but struggling on a daily basis with weaknesses of all kinds. They lift holy hands, sing hallelujah and greet you with a smile. But behind the scenes they know the weaknesses they are contending with.

It becomes a tragedy when people are ignorant of their weakness, or when they pretend that they have none. The devil will always try to bring us down through our weakness. That is why we have to hide ourselves in God that He may show Himself strong on our behalf.

You are only as strong as your worst weakness. A chain is as strong as its weakest link. Suppose you use a chain to, say, tow a broken down car behind your vehicle. If the car is heavy enough, the chain might break. Where will it break? At the weakest link. The point being this: Suppose you made a chain with ten links, nine links of case-hardened steel, and one link of tin. Then you try to pull a heavy object with it. What will happen? The tin link will break. It doesn't matter how strong the other nine links are. If just one link is weak, the chain will break. The overall strength of a chain, is not the strength of the strongest link, or even of the average link. The overall strength of a chain is the strength of the weakest link.

A church organisation is only as strong or as powerful as its weakest aspect. The organisation might be very strong in finances and resources management, but weak in evangelism, worship and prayer – or vice versa. These areas of weakness will determine the overall strength of the church. In other words, one weak aspect can cause an entire organisation to fail. A ministry team or group is only as strong as its weakest member. The overall strength is not the prayerfulness of majority of the members but the prayerlessness of that one member who chooses not to pray. One weak person can cause an entire team to fail, meaning, the individual's laziness or incompetence or whatever flaw, will make the team fail no matter how strong everyone else is, or how well everyone else does.

Imagine that you had ten people running a race as a team, and the team had to finish together, at the same time. No matter how fast your FASTEST person is; he cannot finish until EVERYONE else finishes at the same time. Therefore the SLOWEST person on the team affects the speed of the fastest runner. The

ENTIRE team is as slow as the slowest person. The slow person is the "weakest link".

According to the narrative of Joshua 7, Achan the son of Carmi pillaged gold, silver, and a "beautiful Babylonian garment" from Jericho, in contravention of Joshua's directive that "all the silver, and gold, and vessels of brass and iron, are consecrated unto the Lord: they shall come into the treasury of the Lord" (Joshua 6:19). Although the account suggests that Achan personally was guilty of coveting and taking these spoils, the chapter opens with a statement that the whole community of "the children of Israel [had] committed a trespass" (Joshua 7:1).

This act resulted in the Israelites being collectively punished by God, in that they failed in their first attempt to capture Ai, with about 36 Israelites lives lost. "Achan brought trouble on Israel by violating the ban on taking devoted things." (1 Chronicles 2:7). The lusts of one man led to a defeat in battle, the loss of innocent lives, and the discouragement of an entire nation.

Yield your weaknesses to Christ. He will be strong on your behalf. "Therefore I take pleasure in infirmities, in reproaches, in necessities, in persecutions, in distresses for Christ's sake: for when I am weak, then am I strong." (2 Corinthians 12:10).

"The heroes of faith were commended for their faith. By faith, they quenched the power of fire, escaped the edge of the sword, **were made strong out of weakness**, and became mighty in war." (Hebrews 11:34).

God has promised to strengthen us in our weakness for he understands our weaknesses. "I will seek the lost, and I will bring back the strayed, and I will bind up the injured, and **I will strengthen the weak**." (Ezekiel 34:16). "He gives power to the weak, and to him who has no might he increase strength. Even the youth shall faint and be weary, and young men shall fall exhausted; but they who wait for the LORD shall renew their strength; they shall mount up with wings like eagles; they shall run and not be weary; they shall walk and not faint." (Isaiah 40:29-30).

Jesus understands our weaknesses, for he faced all of the same tests we do, yet he did not sin. So, we can boldly approach the throne of our gracious God, to receive mercy and grace to help us when we need them most. (Hebrews 4:15).

Do not let your weakness hinder your service to God. Do not use it as an excuse. Do not say, 'I am not good enough, I do not speak well, I am not well educated, I am not gifted... etc.' Keep on ministering to the ones considered stronger than you. For in ministering to them, will you find grace and favour to rise above and to overcome your weakness.

Let us consider the example of Abraham and that of his great grandson Joseph. These two disregarded their circumstances and ministered unto others in similar situations to theirs. As a direct result, and consequence of serving God. In spite of their weakness, God remembered them and fulfilled his promises to them. It may have taken many years for the promises to come to pass but the Lord did what He had promised, just as He always does because He is forever faithful.

Abraham: praying for Abimelech's barren women whilst Sarah still remained childless.

Abraham stumbled in a place that he had stumbled before – lying that Sarah was his wife. Instead of trusting God to keep his family together, he devised his own plan to do it. His plan would fail completely. Interestingly, the information Abraham gave was totally factual. Sarah was his half-sister. But it wasn't the whole truth. Abram's intent was clearly to deceive. He was trusting in his deception to protect him instead of trusting in the Lord.

Despite Abraham's failure to really trust God in the situation, God did not abandon him. He would not let Abimelech touch Sarah. That womb was sacred. For it was going to bring forth the son of promise, who would eventually bring forth God's Messiah. God would not leave this matter up to man.

We need to take notice of God's amazing grace: He instructed the deceiver to pray for the deceived! God did not regard Abraham from the standing point of his weakness. He saw him as a prophet – as a man who was carrying His Word. Even though Abraham had stumbled one more time, to God, he was still a prophet and a man of powerful prayer. God's mercy did not leave Abraham, even though Abraham didn't trust God the way he should.

Abraham did not question God why he had to pray for other barren women whilst his wife remained barren. Abraham prayed to God; and God healed Abimelech, his wife, and his female servants. Then they bore children; for the Lord had closed up all the wombs of the house of Abimelech because of Sarah, Abraham's wife.

What a humbling experience it must have been for Abraham to intercede on behalf of Abimelech. If I was the one, a deep sense of unworthiness would have come over me. It was surely not his righteousness which was the basis for the divine healing. Any time that we are used of God, it is solely because of the grace of God.

This marked the beginning of Abraham's and Sarah's next chapter – quite literally because Genesis 21 starts with the following declaration: "The LORD kept his word and did for Sarah exactly what he had promised. She became pregnant, and she gave birth to a son for Abraham in his old age. This happened at just the time God had said it would. And Abraham named their son Isaac." The promise was not fulfilled because Abraham was perfect in his obedience. Far from it; the promise was fulfilled because God was faithful to His Word, even in the light of Abraham's weakness.

Joseph: interpreting other peoples' dreams while his still remained unfulfilled

If there are men who have gone through the school of hard knocks, Joseph must be a high profile alumnus. I sometimes try to picture him being captured in the excitement and imagination brought about by his dreams, only for him to be jeered and deflated by his folks. A dream or a vision with a prophetic dimension or a promising outcome to it, will surely stimulate the anticipation of anyone. This is because it inspires hope of a better future. On the other hand, a dream or a vision that fails to become a reality, crushes ones hope and leads to disappointment. "Hope deferred makes the heart sick, but a dream fulfilled is a tree of life." (Proverbs 13:12).

Many people, crushed by disappointment, have lost hope that dreams will ever become a reality, because of the antithetic nature of their present circumstances. They now live in fear of dreaming again, to mitigate chances of further disappointment.

Joseph had the gifts of prophecy and interpretation of dreams. But he was betrayed in the worst way by the very people, whom he thought would love and protect him. He remained close to the Lord, and found himself working for Potiphar. Things started picking up, Potiphar liked him and gave him charge over all things. Then Potiphar's wife tried to seduce him and get him to sleep with her. Joseph did the right thing and refused, but then found himself framed by the spurned woman and thrown into the prison, the victim of yet another injustice.

He still didn't give up on the Lord, and soon after became well-liked and promoted even in prison. When in prison, a divine opportunity presented itself. He made an appeal to someone capable of ending his plight, the Pharaoh's chief butler. Like Joseph, the butler had fallen upon hard times and had himself been imprisoned. Joseph interpreted the butler's dream that described how the Pharaoh would soon free him. When the dream came true, and the butler was about to be released, Joseph entreated him to intercede on his behalf before Pharaoh. The butler said he would, but forgot. Joseph waited, and waited, and ended up staying in prison for another 2 years. The butler had forgotten all about him.

Probably, in the midst of that long wait, Joseph battled with disappointment. He had done everything right, but no real reward seemed to be coming. Finally, the Pharaoh had a dream. When the Pharaoh's advisers failed to interpret these dreams, the cup-bearer remembered Joseph. Joseph was then summoned. He interpreted the dream and advised the Pharaoh on what to do.

When it seemed like nothing was ever going to happen, Joseph got summoned before Pharaoh to interpret a distressing dream of Pharaoh's that no one else could interpret. Joseph attributed the interpretation to God. And this time he found himself promoted and given charge over all of Egypt, second only to Pharaoh himself. He got a wife, then sons, and later on the opportunity to preserve the lives of his father and brothers in the famine – His own dream was fulfilled.

As you watch days, months or years go by, choose to focus on guarding your heart from becoming bitter. Even though the disappointments along the way to our destiny are bitter, God turns them into stepping-stones for us to fulfil our destiny.

If Joseph had sat back and wallowed in self-pity and refused to interpret the butler's dream, the Pharaoh would probably not have known about him and his gifts. Do not let an unrealised dream, vision or unfulfilled promise become a stumbling block. Instead, purpose to view it as a stepping-stone, taking you deeper into the will and purpose of God.

When we yield and serve God in our weaknesses, the power of God is manifested. In 1 Corinthians 2:3-5, Paul says, "I came to you in weakness, with great fear and trembling. My message and my preaching were not with wise and persuasive words, but with a demonstration of the Spirit's power, so that your faith might not rest on human wisdom, but on God's power. Let God glorify himself through your weakness.

THE JOSHUA SEASON

"So the Lord gave Israel all the land he had solemnly promised to their ancestors, and they conquered it and lived in it. The Lord made them secure, in fulfilment of all he had solemnly promised their ancestors. None of their enemies could resist them. Not one of the Lord's faithful promises to the family of Israel was left unfulfilled; every one was realized."

Joshua 21:43 – 45

One of the main themes of the book of Joshua is to show God's faithfulness to His promises; that He had done for Israel exactly what He had promised. After the death of Moses, God spoke directly to Joshua and commissioned him, assigning him the mandate to lead the Israelites into Canaan. God first addressed the Elephant in the room: the death of His servant Moses, Joshua's mentor and spiritual father. In essence, God was reminding Joshua that even though Moses' season was officially over, the promise to possess the Promised Land still remained. Moses was dead but God was alive.

It is important to take note that the anointing that brings you out of Egypt is not necessarily the same anointing that takes you into the Promised Land. The Bible says, The Holy Spirit is constantly transforming us from glory to glory (2 Corinthians 3:18) and that God gives us grace upon grace (John 1:16). In other words, you need more grace, upon the grace that sustained you in the wilderness, to possess the land.

A new season calls for a fresh anointing and renewed minds. A new season means new wineskins for new wine. No one puts new wine into old wineskins. If this happens, the new wine will burst the skins, the wine will spill, and the wineskins will be ruined. (Luke 5:38 – 39).

Moses Season

The real epiphany for this season starts at the backside of the desert. It is characterised by: Coming out of Egypt's bondage – (salvation), Crossing the Red Sea (water baptism), the pillar of cloud and fire (baptism by the Holy Spirit), The wilderness (testing, preparation and transformation) and the Mountain (seeking the face of God).

It is during this season when we become separated unto the Lord and yearn for the intimacy of God's presence. Moses was at the mountain 40 days and 40 nights and he experienced the glory of God (Ex 24:16-17).

The Moses season is also a season of faithful service to God. (Hebrews 3: 5). During this season, we are not concerned about publicity and recognition. We are passionate about one thing: walking in obedience to the living God.

Joshua Season

When Joshua takes the stage, there is a paradigm shift. The message is simple and clear, that the wilderness season is over; it is time to enter in and possess. It is time to stop depending on manna and to start enjoying milk and honey instead.

Joshua season is characterised by an outpouring of a conquering anointing. It is a season of God's supernatural victory. Because the Lord will fight all your battles (Joshua 10:12-14).

In Canaan, were enemies and forces much mightier than Israel? yet these enemies were a defeated foe even before Israel ever struck a blow. Why? Because the victory of Israel lay not in its own skill or power, but in the power and might of *Yahweh* their God.

Please note that every season has its battles. The demons of the next season, standing in the way of your inheritance, might be more foolish than anything you have dealt with before; but be of good cheer because the battle belongs to the Lord.

This is the time for the body of Christ to engage in battles, that will recapture everything that was stolen by the enemy, both in the church and in culture.

Joshua season is also characterised by wielding of righteous authority. When Moses came to the burning bush, God said take off your shoes for your feet are standing on holy ground. But unto Joshua He said "Every place that the sole of your foot shall tread upon, that I have given unto you" (Joshua 1:3).

In other words, every place Joshua set foot became holy ground; for the Lord had already gone before him and He has given the same to Joshua.

It is a season of rising up in righteousness and authority so as to complete the assignment; to finish the task and to inherit the land. God is calling us to boldly stand on His Word like Joshua, and no man or woman will able to stand in resistance before us.

"For this reason, He is the mediator of a new covenant, so that, since a death has taken place for the redemption of the transgressions that were committed under the first covenant, those who have been called may receive the promise of the eternal inheritance."

Hebrews 9:15

Printed in Great Britain
by Amazon